Bees!

Written by Mio Debnam

Collins

Buzz! Buzz!

See the bees in the garden.

The bee needs food.

She looks for sap.

sap

Sap!

She zigzags to tell all the bees.

7

The sun is high.

The bee is hot!

She fans her wings.

It keeps the air cool.

Food for bees ...

beekeeper

12

... is food for us too!

Bees

After reading

Letters and Sounds: Phase 3

Word count: 50

Focus phonemes: /ee/ /igh/ /oo/ /oo/ /ar/ /or/ /air/ /er/

Common exception words: the, she, all

Curriculum links: Understanding the World

Early learning goals: Reading: read and understand simple sentences; use phonic knowledge to decode regular words and read them aloud accurately; read some common irregular words

Developing fluency

- Your child may enjoy hearing you read the book.
- Take turns to read a page, and remind your child to look out for exclamation marks, and to read these sentences with extra excitement or surprise.

Phonic practice

- Ask your child to reread page 3, then point to **see** and ask: Which letters make the "ee" sound? (*ee*).
- Point to **garden** and ask: Which letters make the "ar" sound? (*ar*)
- Turn to page 8, then pages 12 and 13. Ask your child to find the two or three letters that make each of these sounds:

  /igh/ (*high*)   /oo/ (*food*/*too*)   /er/ (*beekeeper*)   /or/ (*for*)

Extending vocabulary

- Read the text on pages 4 and 5. Point to **she** and say: What is the opposite of **she**? (*he*) Talk about the meanings of **she** and "he". Explain that worker bees are all female which is why they are called **she** in the book. The female worker bees look after the hive and collect sap (nectar) and feed the other bees. Explain that a "he" or male bee is called a drone, and their job is to stay in the hive until they fly off to mate with a queen bee from another hive.
- Discuss the meaning of words linked to bees, including: hive, mate, queen, nectar, honey, **beekeeper**. Help your child to look the words up in an age-appropriate dictionary, if necessary.